Luciferian Society

&

The Wall

By Joseph Dulmage

A tribute to Eleazar, the great swordsman.
Bold as a lion, he led me behind the wall made
with tempered morter.

2 Samuel 23: 10 *He arose, and smote the
Philistines until his hand was weary, and his hand
clave unto the sword: and the LORD wrought a great
victory that day; and the people returned after him
only to spoil.*

Index

Contents

Preface

Scripture moves through human history like the breath of God. The evolution of language does not render God's words fallible, nor does it negate his power to preserve. An inerrant Bible exceeds all doctrines of Christianity, transcending the deity of Jesus Christ, his virgin birth, his death, or his resurrection; for God's words bring these truths to us. God literally magnifies his written word above his name. God's words project himself. Inspiration without preservation would be worthless.

Psalms 138:2 *I will worship toward thy holy temple, and praise thy name for thy lovingkindness and for thy truth: for thou hast magnified thy word above all thy name.*

Psalms 12:6-7 *The words of the LORD are pure words: as silver tried in a furnace of earth, purified seven times.* *7* *Thou shalt keep them, O LORD, thou shalt preserve them from this generation for ever.*

John 5:39 *Search the scriptures; for in them ye think ye have eternal life: and they are they which testify of me.*

The Wall

Allegorical Commentary
Ezekiel Chapter Thirteen

Ezekiel 13:6 *They have seen vanity and lying divination, saying, The LORD saith: and the LORD hath not sent them: and they have made others to hope that they would confirm the word.*

A peculiar city lived within a hostile country. People inside the city sang songs and possessed great joy in their hearts. The people in the hostile country hated the peculiar city, because her citizens believed someone they refused. They hated her songs, because they couldn't catch the tune. But most of all, they hated the joy her citizens possessed in their hearts.

The peculiar city's citizens continually invited the hostile country's residents to join them. Every now and then, some residents accepted and moved into the peculiar city. Upon entry, the immigration authority furnished males and females a suit of armour and a red sword. Throughout history, many valiant soldiers fought bravely to defend the peculiar city, but beyond all doubt, the city's salvation owed allegiance to her wall. The wall, itself, protected the city and shown as a beacon of hope and safety, calling people up out of the hostile country.

The wall was built with stones. One stone upon another set in distinct lines or layers. Tempered red morter enclosed each stone, cementing them together. Although some sections of the wall were much older than other sections, it stayed remarkably constant. Stone upon stone, line upon line, the wall formed a perfect wholeness, an unbroken strength. Any weapon the hostile country used against the wall proved ineffective. The wall always held true.

As the peculiar city's population grew and prospered, they developed great learning centers which studied all aspects of life. Professors studied the wall with utmost scrutiny. Scholars pursued extensive mining expeditions seeking treasure to fund the learning centers and the cost of the mines.

One day a stranger entered the peculiar city. Possessing intelligence above common citizens, he found communion in the learning centers. And therein he expressed concern about the wall. He warned softly. "Are the stones not small and weak? Can the red morter holding the stones protect us in this day and age? Our mining expeditions uncover stones much larger and stronger than those used in the old wall. Learned and wise men believe these bigger and stronger stones are also wall stones, no doubt once used to defend our beloved city. Should we not repair the wall, and protect the wellbeing of our citizens?" Sagacious scholars agreed, and efforts began to repair the wall.

At first, common citizens did not hear concerns about the wall because scholars only whispered warnings in the learning centers. The citizens never questioned the wall's integrity, for it always protected them without fail. They lived grateful and secure. But now things began to change. More mining expeditions took place and scholars found more stones. In fact, with so many stones; they abandoned their idea to repair the wall and decided to build a whole new wall. Academics were ecstatic.

And they said one to another, "Go to, let us make a stronger more reliable wall in front of the old wall. This will expand our territory inside the hostile country. We need not take down the old wall, for it served us reliably for centuries, but let it stand alone. Besides, the people do not understand the stones as we do, and they may frighten if we tear it down. But once they see the new wall with larger and stronger stones, and the land gained is good for prospering, they will move their houses from behind the old wall and settle behind the new wall."

At the new wall's completion, a great dedication ceremony took place. Scholars from nearly all learning centers participated in the glorious occasion. The new wall loomed magnificent. The stones, indeed, were larger and appeared stronger than stones in the old wall. And they were not placed line upon line, but rather, in impressive blocks or sections. These sections, held together with beautiful pink untempered morter, developed by the finest wall custodians from the best learning centers. As the professors and scholars stood with their backs against the old wall, the stranger went forward and concluded the dedication.

With a smile on his face and satisfaction in his eyes, the stranger spread his arms as if to embrace all the people. "Brothers and Sisters, fellow custodians of the wall; we who consecrate our lives to preserve and protect the peculiar city are especially pleased today. Before us stands the fruit of our labors. While our accomplishments shine brightly, let us humbly acknowledge we only improve and continue the legacy of wall preservation. Today, our humility rewards us with a greater, stronger wall than has ever stood." The stranger turned and raised his arms in worship like gesture to the huge pink monument; he spoke in a powerful voice, "Behold thy wall, O peculiar city, which has brought thee up from the hostile country and preserves your souls."

So impressive was the new wall, even common citizens began questioning the old wall's security. They said, "Maybe the old wall should be taken down? Look how beautiful the country is between us and the new wall. Since its stones are bigger and stronger, surely it's safe to move our houses to the country. The wall custodians love the peculiar city and would never put us in harm's way."

Some citizens, however, did not trust the new wall. Mr. Eleazar, the great swordsman, observed the pink morter did not enclose each and every stone. And pink morter showed cracks almost immediately, while the tempered, red morter in the old wall never cracked. He asked why pink morter was untempered. And even though the stones were bigger in the new wall, Mr. Eleazar questioned if this truly made it stronger.

Alas, the new wall's custodians merely sighed and dismissed his questions with a wave of their hands and a shaking of their heads, for they understood Mr. Eleazar knew very little about stones and even less about morter. So faith in the new wall became stronger and stronger, and the number of citizens who believed in the old wall became less and less.

Mining expeditions continued, accumulating so many stones they built more walls using untempered morter. And all new walls promised to be stronger and better than the old wall. Most importantly, custodians built each wall in front of their previous construction; thus extending the peculiar city's limits further and further into hostile country.

One of the most fascinating mining expeditions dug beneath the old wall and found its very foundation. "This," said scholars, "must be entirely unearthed, for the foundation is stronger and better than the wall above the ground."

"But why?" asked Mr. Eleazar. "Our enemies attack on ground level and the wall above ground always repels their attacks. And the old wall's visibility steadfastly draws folks from the hostile country to join our happy citizenry. The foundation supports the old wall exactly as intended and belongs where it is?"

Alas, wall custodians merely sighed and dismissed his comments with a wave of their hands and a shaking of their heads, for they understood Mr. Eleazar knew very little about stones and even less about foundations. So faith in the new walls became stronger and stronger, and the number of citizens who believed in the old wall became less and less.

Eventually custodians renewed efforts to take down the old wall, but no matter how hard they tried, the old wall remained unmovable. They said, therefore, "let us ignore the old wall's persistence the best we can and encourage citizens to move. Soon the people's injudicious trust will instigate a disregard for the old wall."

And since land beyond the old wall looked so prosperous, and with so many new and stronger walls, many citizens moved out from behind the old wall and settled in the newly enclosed areas. All the finest learning centers moved first, and then the people followed.

Mr. Eleazar, still living behind the old wall, observed no one trusting in the new walls owned a red sword. The citizen's sword, in every case, matched the color of the morter in the newer walls. Swords' colors ranged from pink to dull gray. None red.

Darkness settled over the peculiar city and people slept peacefully. When the attack commenced, it actually took citizens living behind the outermost wall completely by surprise. But the enemies looked so small; the citizens hardly cared for the showers of arrows pelting outside their towering gray wall. But each arrow chipped away a piece of morter, and within a few hours the huge wall collapsed. The citizens gray swords broke apart in hand to hand combat, and surrender came quickly. Those not killed were taken prisoner and led back to the interior of the hostile country.

Exuberant over victory, the enemy charged the next wall. Soon that wall fell and citizens suffered the same fate as those before them. Wall after wall fell to the enemy, and fully half the peculiar city's population were either dead or taken captive. Only two walls remained, the great pink wall and the old red wall.

Nearly all learning centers had relocated behind the great pink wall. The custodians stood bravely in front of their institutions with their pink swords drawn. Common citizens, too, held their weapons and prepared for battle. Shower after shower of arrows chipped away at the wall. The sky turned black and a ferocious storm wind blew. Great hailstones fell against the wall, beating the untempered morter to dust. Hundreds of larger and stronger stones fell from the wall crushing many custodians to death. Finally the wall collapsed sending a billowing cloud of pink dust into the air. As the dust settled, it infected the people's eyes. Citizens went blind even as the enemy climbed over the bigger and stronger stones; the slaughter was hideous.

Mr. Eleazar led a group of knights from behind the old wall to meet the enemy. He fought ferociously urging citizens to seek refuge behind the old wall. Mr. Eleazar's red sword blazed like fire, hundreds of the enemy lay dead around him. His eyes met the stranger. The stranger fought without a sword, but held a pouch of darts; he smiled wily at Mr. Eleazar, and then disappeared in pink dust. Mr. Eleazar fought on; he smote the enemy until his hand was weary, and his hand clave unto the sword.

"Fight," yelled Mr. Eleazar. "Fight! Return to the old wall, our mighty fortress, its stones are as silver tried in a furnace of earth, purified seven times.

And preserved forever by our holy and omnipotent God."

But many citizens could not fight. Most were blind, and the pink swords broke easily when arrows hit them. The enemy kept coming, intoxicated with triumph.

Mr. Eleazar's warning alerted many citizens, and he led them back behind the old wall. On top of the stones, he watched in horror as citizens fell in battle. Although light emanated from the old wall, the people wearied themselves in desolate places and could no longer see. They stumbled in obscurity. They moved in darkness and groped for the wall like the blind. They groped as if they had no eyes and stumbled into the mouth of the lion.

Isaiah 59:9-10 Therefore is judgment far from us, neither doth justice overtake us: we wait for light, but behold obscurity; for brightness, but we walk in darkness. 10 We grope for the wall like the blind, and we grope as if we had no eyes: we stumble at noonday as in the night; we are in desolate places as dead men.

1 Peter 5:8 Be sober, be vigilant; because your adversary the devil, as a roaring lion, walketh about, seeking whom he may devour:

End

Wall Glossary

Story notes: Allegorical basis for characters: Subjective interpretation.

Citizen Army:

Christians/2 Timothy 2:4 *No man that warreth entangleth himself with the affairs of this life; that he may please him who hath chosen him to be a soldier.*

Revelation 19:14 *And the armies which were in heaven followed him upon white horses, clothed in fine linen, white and clean.*

Custodians: Scribes

Beware of the Scribes:

Luke 20:46-47 *Beware of the scribes, which desire to walk in long robes, and love greetings in the markets, and the highest seats in the synagogues, and the chief rooms at feasts;* ***47*** *Which devour widows' houses, and for a shew make long prayers: the same shall receive greater damnation.*

Colossians 2:8 *Beware lest any man spoil you through philosophy and vain deceit, after the tradition of men, after the rudiments of the world, and not after Christ.*

Acts 20:29-30 *For I know this, that after my departing shall grievous wolves enter in among you, not sparing the flock.* ***30*** *Also of your own selves shall* *men arise, speaking perverse things, to draw away disciples after them.*

__2 Corinthians 11:13-15__ For such are false apostles, deceitful workers, transforming themselves into the apostles of Christ. __14__ And no marvel; for Satan himself is transformed into an angel of light. __15__ Therefore it is no great thing if his ministers also be transformed as the ministers of righteousness; whose end shall be according to their works.

Babylon: to confuse by mixing.

Mr. Eleazar: Christian pastor warning the sheep about corrupt bibles.

Eleazar (God is helper)

__2 Samuel 23:9-10__ And after him was Eleazar the son of Dodo the Ahohite, one of the three mighty men with David, when they defied the Philistines that were there gathered together to battle, and the men of Israel were gone away: __10__ He arose, and smote the Philistines until his hand was weary, and his hand clave unto the sword: and the LORD wrought a great victory that day; and the people returned after him only to spoil.

Wall made with tempered morter: King James Bible

__Joshua 8:32__ And he wrote there upon the stones a copy of the law of Moses, which he wrote in the presence of the children of Israel.

Isaiah 28:13 But the word of the LORD was unto them precept upon precept, precept upon precept; line upon line, line upon line; here a little, and there a little; that they might go, and fall backward, and be broken, and snared, and taken.

Lamentations 2:18 Their heart cried unto the Lord, O wall of the daughter of Zion, let tears run down like a river day and night: give thyself no rest; let not the apple of thine eye cease.

Walls made with untempered morter-to replace the old wall made with tempered morter: Bibles written to replace the King James Bible

God uses the words untempered morter five times and only in Ezekiel 13.

Corrupted Bibles

Zechariah 5:3-4 Then said he unto me, This is the curse that goeth forth over the face of the whole earth: for every one that stealeth shall be cut off as on this side according to it; and every one that sweareth shall be cut off as on that side according to it. *4* I will bring it forth, saith the LORD of hosts, and it shall enter into the house of the thief, and into the house of him that sweareth falsely by my name: and it shall remain in the midst of his house, and shall consume it with the timber thereof and the stones thereof.

Ezekiel 13:10 Because, even because they have seduced my people, saying, Peace; and there was no peace; and one built up a wall, and, lo, others daubed it with untempered morter:

Ezekiel 13:11 Say unto them which daub it with untempered morter, that it shall fall: there shall be an overflowing shower; and ye, O great hailstones, shall fall; and a stormy wind shall rend it.

Ezekiel 13:14 So will I break down the wall that ye have daubed with untempered morter, and bring it down to the ground, so that the foundation thereof shall be discovered, and it shall fall, and ye shall be consumed in the midst thereof: and ye shall know that I am the LORD.

Ezekiel 13:15 Thus will I accomplish my wrath upon the wall, and upon them that have daubed it with untempered morter, and will say unto you, The wall is no more, neither they that daubed it;

Ezekiel 22:28 And her prophets have daubed them with untempered morter, seeing vanity, and divining lies unto them, saying, Thus saith the Lord GOD, when the LORD hath not spoken.

Zechariah 1:6 But my words and my statutes, which I commanded my servants the prophets, did they not take hold of your fathers? and they returned and said, Like as the LORD of hosts thought to do unto us, according to our ways, and according to our doings, so hath he dealt with us.

Peculiar City:

The Church/Christians

Titus 2:14 *Who gave himself for us, that he might redeem us from all iniquity, and purify unto himself a peculiar people, zealous of good works.*

Hebrews 11:16 *But now they desire a better country, that is, an heavenly: wherefore God is not ashamed to be called their God: for he hath prepared for them a city.*

Suit of Armour:

Ephesians 6:13 *Wherefore take unto you the whole armour of God, that ye may be able to withstand in the evil day, and having done all, to stand.*

Sword: word of God

Ephesians 6:17 And take the helmet of salvation, and the sword of the Spirit, which is the word of God:

Zechariah 2:4-5 *And said unto him, Run, speak to this young man, saying, Jerusalem shall be inhabited as towns without walls for the multitude of men and cattle therein: 5 For I, saith the LORD, will be unto her a wall of fire round about, and will be the glory in the midst of her.*

Isaiah 25:4 *For thou hast been a strength to the poor, a strength to the needy in his distress, a refuge from the storm, a shadow from the heat, when the blast of the terrible ones is as a storm against the wall.*

Isaiah 59:10 *We grope for the wall like the blind, and we grope as if we had no eyes: we stumble at noonday as in the night; we are in desolate places as dead men.*

Ezekiel 13:1-23 *And the word of the LORD came unto me, saying, 2 Son of man, prophesy against the prophets of Israel that prophesy, and say thou unto them that prophesy out of their own hearts, Hear ye the word of the LORD; 3 Thus saith the Lord GOD; Woe unto the foolish prophets, that follow their own spirit, and have seen nothing! 4 O Israel, thy prophets are like the foxes in the deserts. 5 Ye have not gone up into the gaps, neither made up the hedge for the house of Israel to stand in the battle in the day of the LORD. 6 They have seen vanity and lying divination, saying, The LORD saith: and the LORD hath not sent them: and they have made others to hope that they would confirm the word. 7 Have ye not seen a vain vision, and have ye not spoken a lying divination, whereas ye say, The LORD saith it; albeit I have not spoken? 8 Therefore thus saith the Lord GOD; Because ye have spoken vanity, and seen lies, therefore, behold, I am against you, saith the Lord GOD. 9 And mine hand shall be upon the prophets that see vanity, and that divine lies: they shall not be in the assembly of my people, neither shall they be written in the writing of the house of Israel, neither shall they enter into the land of Israel; and ye shall know that I am the Lord GOD. 10 Because, even because they have seduced my people, saying, Peace; and there was no peace; and one built up a wall, and, lo, others daubed it with untempered morter: 11 Say unto them which daub it* with untempered morter, that it shall fall: there shall be an overflowing shower; and ye, O great hailstones, shall fall; and a stormy wind shall rend it. **12** Lo, when the wall is fallen, shall it not be said unto you, Where is the daubing wherewith ye have daubed it? **13** Therefore thus saith the Lord GOD; I will even rend it with a stormy wind in my fury; and there shall be an overflowing shower in mine anger, and great hailstones in my fury to consume it. **14** So will I break down the wall that ye have daubed with untempered morter, and bring it down to the ground, so that the foundation thereof shall be discovered, and it shall fall, and ye shall be consumed in the midst thereof: and ye shall know that I am the LORD. **15** Thus will I accomplish my wrath upon the wall, and upon them that have daubed it with untempered morter, and will say unto you, The wall is no more, neither they that daubed it; **16** To wit, the prophets of Israel which prophesy concerning Jerusalem, and which see visions of peace for her, and there is no peace, saith the Lord GOD. **17** Likewise, thou son of man, set thy face against the daughters of thy people, which prophesy out of their own heart; and prophesy thou against them, **18** And say, Thus saith the Lord GOD; Woe to the women that sew pillows to all armholes, and make kerchiefs upon the head of every stature to hunt souls! Will ye hunt the souls of my people, and will ye save the souls alive that come unto you? **19** And will ye pollute me among my people for handfuls of barley and for pieces of bread, to slay the souls that should not die, and to save the souls alive that should not live, by your lying to my people that hear your lies? **20** Wherefore thus saith the Lord GOD; Behold, I am against your pillows, *wherewith ye there hunt the souls to make them fly, and I will tear them from your arms, and will let the souls go, even the souls that ye hunt to make them fly. 21 Your kerchiefs also will I tear, and deliver my people out of your hand, and they shall be no more in your hand to be hunted; and ye shall know that I am the LORD. 22 Because with lies ye have made the heart of the righteous sad, whom I have not made sad; and strengthened the hands of the wicked, that he should not return from his wicked way, by promising him life: 23 Therefore ye shall see no more vanity, nor divine divinations: for I will deliver my people out of your hand: and ye shall know that I am the LORD.*

The Luciferian Society

An allegorical tale

Matthew 22:29 *Jesus answered and said unto them, Ye do err, not knowing the scriptures, nor the power of God.*

Mrs. Margaret Thompson waited for her coffee cake and read the message on the bulletin board in the town bakery.

Luciferian Society Meeting:
Saturday 6:00 PM
Where: Master's Church 333 Onyx Road
Topic: Morality and Ignorance
Christians, Bring your Bibles.

"Frank," said Margaret turning toward the counter, "did you happen to see who posted this announcement about a Luciferian Society?"

"Yes," answered Frank, as he boxed the coffee cake, "the new minister of Master's Church. Every morning, for the last two weeks he's been in to buy doughnuts for his staff. Heck of a nice guy."

"Did he say anything about it to you?"

"Not really," said Frank. "He asked if he could post a community message. And I said that's what the board is for. Then we talked about the front-page story in the news today. You know the one about the murderer who got out of prison after serving only two years. Boy, was he ever mad about that. He said

22

America doesn't have a justice system anymore; it only has a legal system. He said our courts sacrifice justice for law. And all for the love of money. I'm telling you, Margaret, the guy, really made a lot of sense. I might even go to his church this Sunday. And you know me; I haven't been to church in years."

"But what is this Luciferian Society?" asked Margaret. "Why would a minister hold a meeting like that?"

"Hey," said Frank, "How should I know? Why are you sounding so mad, anyway?"

"Do you know who Lucifer is?" asked Margaret.

"Some angel, isn't he?" said Frank.

"Frank, the Bible says Lucifer is the devil. It doesn't make sense a Christian minister has a Luciferian Society."

"I don't know anything about it," said Frank. "But don't jump to any conclusions. I'm telling you the guy is OK."

Margaret paid for the coffee cake and hurried to her car. When she arrived home, she called her pastor, Bob Leaven.

"Yes, Margaret," said Pastor Leaven, "I share your concerns. Matter of fact, there's an invitation to the meeting on my desk right now. Came in the mail today. Apparently, this new minister," he paused and picked up the letter, "his name is Alexander Burehc, sent an invitation to every pastor and clergyman in town.

"Dr. Jehudi, Pastor of Dan Baptist, called me about half an hour ago. He said Reverend Burehc came to his office and asked him to come. That's what having a congregation over a thousand will do for you. Us little guys get a letter, and the big boys get a personal invitation. Dr. Jehudi says he's one of the nicest men he's ever met, very interesting and extremely intelligent too."

"Do you plan on going?" asked Margaret.

"Yes, Margaret, I do plan to attend. I'm curious. Besides, I can't remember Dr. Jehudi ever being impressed by anyone. As for the Luciferian Society, we'll just have to wait and hear his explanation."

By 5:30 PM on Saturday 300 hundred cars filled the Master's Church parking lot. Inside the building, people mingled about, anxiously awaiting the meeting. Dr. Jehudi and fifty members from Dan Baptist sat near the front of the church. A group of Methodists sat behind them. Across the aisle from the Baptists, Father Micah and several dozen people from St. Mary's filled the front pews. Representatives from numerous home churches, as well as newer independent Pentecostal churches from Admah County inhabited the auditorium's balcony.

Reverend Burehc walked among the people, introducing himself and extending a warm welcome. So affable and charming, he even put Margaret Thompson at ease. At precisely 6:00 PM, he went to the platform and stood behind the podium.

"Ladies and Gentlemen, if everyone finds a seat we shall begin. It's a beautiful summer evening, and I'm sure no one wants to be kept inside very long."

The crowd shuffled as those standing quickly found a seat. "Thank you for such prompt cooperation," said Burehc. His deep, resonant voice carried well in the huge room. "I'll begin by saying how much I've enjoyed meeting many of you this week. And for those whom I have not met, I can only say the pleasure still awaits me. I moved into town less than a month ago; already I feel wonderfully at home.

"This evening's topic concerns morality and ignorance. As concerned citizens, we see the

25

appalling ravages of lawlessness and the decay of moral values. As believers, we grieve at our own nation's and the world's rapid descent away from godliness. But I am not without hope; I believe the faithful can fulfill our Master's mission. The bible tells us judgment begins at the house of God. And this means judgment begins with us. Yes, brothers and sisters, a great challenge lies before us. There is a good crowd here tonight, yet I hoped such a topic would intrigue many more."

"Maybe the name of your society kept them away?" said someone loudly.

"Ah," said Burehc, "perhaps you are right? Which brings us to the second topic of our discussion, ignorance. No doubt a Luciferian Society meeting in a local church alarmed many of you. But why? Why the apprehension over a mere name?"

"Because Lucifer is the devil," said a gentleman in the first row.

"Is he really?" said Burehc. Scanning the congregation, his eyes seemed to meet them all- one at a time. "Before addressing this issue directly, I shall impose upon the goodwill of our most distinguished citizens. Our community's religious leadership brings an exceptional degree of scholarship, wisdom, and piety to our gathering. Among us reside men well equipped to answer any theological question."

Burehc stopped speaking, distracted by the rear doors opening and the entrance of Brother

Antipas, pastor of a Baptist church just outside the city limits.

"Would all clergymen," Burehc continued, "please come to the front of the auditorium?" He gestured to his left on the platform where fourteen chairs sat empty.

Dr. Jehudi and Father Micah stood first. The crowd responded with applause. Soon all the ministers walked toward the front. Pastor Antipas was the last man down. Burehc eyed him warily when he pulled his chair away from the group before sitting.

"So Lucifer is the devil," repeated Burehc. "May I inquire of the gentleman who made the comment, where he obtained such an accusation?"

"Why, from the Bible, of course," said the man. "I'm not sure just where, but it's in there."

"How many of you brought bibles, tonight?" asked Burehc. About three hundred people raised their hands, some waving bibles.

Reverend Malchus, a Methodist minister, rose to his feet. "The name Lucifer is found in Isaiah 14:12."

"Thank you, Reverend Malchus," said Burehc.

The room filled with soft swishing sounds as pages turned. Some heads nodded in affirmation, yet most people looked bewildered.

"What you are discovering," said Burehc, "Lucifer is not found in all your bibles. Many translations call the person the *Morning Star or Day Star.*

"Not the King James Bible," said Antipas.

"Thank you, Pastor," said Burehc. "Antipas is correct. The King James Bible translates the name Lucifer; most versions, however, replace the name Lucifer with the morning star. Perhaps Dr. Jehudi could explain?"

"Certainly," said Jehudi. He rose and removed his eyeglasses. "Reverend Burehc correctly states, the name Lucifer is translated *morning star, or Day Star* (or some similar variant) in the newer bibles. We must understand the King James Bible, usually provides fine and reliable renderings of the holy writ; however, since that 1611 translation, scholars have accessed far older and more accurate manuscripts. The newer bible versions translate from those manuscripts. This accounts for the occasional and minor discrepancies found within our bibles. Especially with the New Testament, modern scholars are not limited to the Greek texts from whence came the King James."

"Ably addressed in layman's terms, Dr. Jehudi," said Burehc. "I am very pleased Christians still care what bibles say. Although our bibles are reliable, we must recognize our need for qualified scholars to guide and help us with interpretation. Could the ministers recommend the most accurate English bible for this day and age?"

There was a brief discussion among the panel of thirteen church leaders. "You have asked a very important question," said Jehudi. "All of us believe in the inerrancy of the original manuscripts, yet we also acknowledge translation difficulties and human error. Human languages evolve constantly necessitating scribal revision. God continually calls able men to watch over his words; therefore we recognize many excellent versions available today.

"Excuse me," interrupted Antipas, "Concerning the inerrancy of the original manuscripts. Do any original manuscripts exist today?"

"Why, er, ahh, well-- actually, no they do not," answered Jehudi. He seemed surprised at the question.

"Then," said Antipas, "just so all Christians understand, when scholars and church leaders say they believe in the inerrancy of the original manuscripts, they are saying they believe in something that doesn't even exist. In truth, they do not believe any bible we have today is inerrant."

"As I was saying," continued Dr. Jehudi, his composure regained, but clearly annoyed by Antipas, "even though centuries and centuries transpire, and vast changes in language has occurred since the penning of the original autographs, the bible still maintains the integrity of God's words. And we believe ancient copies of manuscripts, although flawed, are mostly preserved. This educated position is held by nearly every Christian college, seminary, scholar, and minister living today."

"What he's saying," said Antipas addressing the people "The vast majority of Christian scholars, professors, and ministers believe their bible is not perfectly preserved, but contains errors."

All the ministers, now visibly agitated with Pastor Antipas.

Jehudi coughed, clearing his throat, "AS I was attempting to explain, although many fine translations exist, those of us rational enough to offer reasonable opinions, recommend two English translations, *The New American Standard Version* (NASV) and the *New International Version (NIV)*. A great many scholars give the NIV a bit of an edge. I personally believe the NASV to be the finest of all English bibles. I do, however, recognize scores of worthy translations. (With promise of many more to come.) Modern bibles consider the evolution of language, and have corrected the archaic and unrecognized words found in the older and less accurate King James Bible."

"Thank you gentlemen," said Burehc, "Your consensus is wise, balanced, and well-articulated in spite of the adversity among us." Stooping down, Burehc retrieved a small stack of bibles from inside the podium. "I will now read the infamous Lucifer passage as it appears in the King James Bible. This followed by readings from several other bibles. I encourage this congregation (and readers) to verify renderings in their own bibles here and at home.

Isaiah 14:12 King James Bible

***How art thou fallen from heaven, O
Lucifer, son of the morning! how art thou cut
down to the ground, which didst weaken the
nations!***

*Isaiah 14:12 How you have fallen from heaven,
O morning star, son of the dawn! You have been cast
down to the earth, you who once laid low the nations*

*Isaiah 14:12 How art thou fallen from heaven,
O day-star, son of the morning! how art thou cut
down to the ground, that didst lay low the nations!*

*Isaiah 14:12 How you have fallen from heaven,
O star of the morning, son of the dawn! You have
been cut down to the earth, You who have weakened
the nations!*

"I chose the name Lucifer for my society
because no other name stands so alone. Lucifer
means 'light bearer or the shining one'. Ironically, the
one whose very name brings light and revelation
remains shrouded in darkness. Lucifer, the antithesis
of ignorance, must ceaselessly fight against
ignorance. And that fight, brothers and sisters, is our
fight. Today the world literally inhabits darkness.
Societies' moral fabric unravels before our eyes.
Ignorance toward our Master's words abounds in
education and the churches. Since Judgment begins
at the house of God, let us judge ourselves with
truths found in ancient manuscripts. Armed with
truth, we can serve the Master with power.

"Yea hath God said, Christian scholarship
concludes the translation of Lucifer incorrect? Do not

ignore counsel from the very men you believe God calls into service. Are these men not shepherds of your faith? Do they not watch for your souls? If the Lucifer translation is an error, let us correct it. When knowledge reveals the morning star is fallen, let us not name the morning star Lucifer and imagine him the devil."

Margaret Thompson raised her hand.

"Yes, Sister," said Burehc.

"I'd like to read a verse and then ask a question."

"Proceed," said Burehc.

"I am reading from the King James Bible, in book of Revelation."

Revelation 22:16 *I Jesus have sent mine angel to testify unto you these things in the churches. I am the root and the offspring of David, and the bright and morning star.*

"Jesus Christ is the morning star. Comparing scripture with scripture, is Jesus the one who fell from heaven?"

"That's exactly what numerous versions teach!" Antipas said quite loudly.

"Pastor Antipas," said Burehc, "you sound so angry. You act as though we commit grave injustice. Participating in an open forum discussing scriptures with all major Christian denominations present, should not upset you. I have gone to great lengths to exercise charity and fairness. Whether you like it or not, the great majority of Christendom, including your own denomination's leading theologians, do not hold the King James only position."

"May I take the lady's question?" Asked Dr. Jehudi with his hand politely raised.

"Please do," said Burehc.

"Once again a little knowledge illuminates the problem. We must understand Isaiah 14 speaks only of an earthly king. Here the morning star is a king in Babylon. Some scholars erroneously applied the passage to a heavenly personage."

Dr. Demetrius, pastor of Christian Babylon Temple, raised his hand. Burehc acknowledged him with a nod. "Dr. Demetrius, you have the floor."

"In my opinion," said Demetrius, "this theological theory about a human king in Babylon is stretching things. I mean, the verse says the morning star fell from heaven. How could a Babylonian king fall from heaven? Furthermore, Jesus himself declares that he is the morning star. I see no logical (or scriptural) reason to doubt what Jesus says.

"Christians who belong to older- more fundamental fellowships, have a very hard time admitting when they're wrong. As the eloquent Dr. Jehudi already stated, scholars possess more accurate biblical manuscripts today than they did centuries ago. Therefore, we should not be shocked if some ancient religious doctrines need revision, even when those teachings concern Jesus Christ.

"I applaud Reverend Burehc for setting up this meeting and his efforts to help society. I also applaud ministers willing to sit down with one another and discuss our doctrines in a unified and ecumenical manner. After all is said and done, don't' we serve the same Master? Today, we take significant steps toward restoring godly morality in our community. Truly, judgment in the house of God has begun."

"Thank you very much, Dr. Demetrius," said Burehc.

Professor Coppersmith, the eldest minister, rose slowly to his feet. He had served as dean of theology and church history with a major Christian university for twenty years.

"Professor Coppersmith, I was hoping we would hear from you," said Burehc.

"Throughout my life," said the professor, I notice Christians incessantly blaming someone else for their own problems as well as their country's problems. Historically, this blame is not limited to flesh and blood; Christians often blame the devil. Even today, it is very common to hear religious people talking about a coming antichrist. And how the devil is orchestrating political dilemmas and evil conspiracies worldwide. This is nothing more than a subconscious attempt to blame even future negative world situations on a devil, or an imaginary Lucifer.

The bible does indeed speak of a beast and an antichrist. I should like to read you the passage which reveals his identity. Again we must appeal to the most accurate manuscripts.

My bible translates Revelation 13:18 as follows: *This calls for wisdom: let him who has understanding reckon the number of the beast, for it is a human number, its number is six hundred and sixty-six.*

In this case wisdom is needed: Let the person who has understanding calculate the total of the beast, since it is a human multitude, and the sum of the multitude is 600, 60, and six.

Revelation 13:18 This calls for wisdom: let him who has understanding reckon the number of the beast, for it is a human number, its number is six hundred and sixty-six.

"Has God truly said the beast is an individual? I tell you NO! The beast is humanity. The great evil is within us. We are all numbered as antichrist. As we judge ourselves, we must repent of ancient doctrines which confuse and divide the brotherhood. Love is the answer. Oh, when will God's children learn to love one another? When will all Christians learn to believe our bibles for what they say, and stop embracing ancient denominational, or fundamentally divisive doctrines?"

Professor Coppersmith sat down; Antipas stood up, his penetrating eyes fastened to Burehc's own stare.

"You wish to speak, Antipas," said Burehc.

"I do," said Antipas.

"You have the floor," said Burehc with a sigh.

"The last two gentlemen reached inevitable, logical conclusions," said Antipas ignoring the glares of the ministers. "Dr. Demetrius and Professor Coppersmith accept the authority of bibles produced by prideful, misdirected scholarship. They believe only in the inerrancy of original manuscripts, which do not even exist, therefore they have no final authority. As you already know, I believe the final authority is the King James Bible. Therefore, I reject any manuscript declaring the morning star fell from heaven. My morning star is not fallen. Nor is antichrist mankind. I read to you from the word of God, the King James Bible.

Revelation 13:18 King James Bible Here is wisdom. Let him that hath understanding count the number of the beast: for it is the number of a man; and his number is Six hundred threescore and six.

"So what is it Christian? Is the beast a man, or is mankind the beast? Is the fallen one Lucifer or the morning star? What a tragedy if you do not know. When anyone looks at the same verse in two different bibles, and each bible says something different, one may conclude them both wrong, but it insults logic to say they are both correct. Christians need exact information. A generally reliable verse, or scripture containing the gist of the truth, settles nothing. Where is a Christian's final authority?

"When a church or any institution asserts: *We believe in the inerrancy of the original manuscripts.* And then, under scrutiny, quietly admit the original manuscripts no longer exist. What does this mean? It is an answer more suited to modern politicians trying to avoid (or spin) a question. Such a statement is declared boldly in hopes their audience interprets it to mean they believe the bible is without error. But they do not believe any existing bible is without error. Ask them. Such a statement allows them to correct bibles as they see fit with statements such as: *In the Greek the verse really means...; In the original manuscripts of the Hebrew...A more accurate translation would be...; blah, blah, blah.*

"Historically, the main division between Protestant Christianity and Roman Catholicism was Protestants believed the bible to be the final authority, while Catholics believe the final authority is their church. Today there is little difference between the two groups. Average bible students are bewildered with all the different bible versions. They are taught to accept scholars' opinions for the correct interpretation of ancient manuscripts. Today, theologians and professors are the Protestants' (and Baptists') priests and cardinals. The bible, as their final authority, no longer exists. Scripture infallibility has been reasoned away.

"Christians who believe the King James Bible is God's word without error -are considered uneducated, misguided, and even trouble makers. Yet we are not ignorant to manuscript evidence. We, too, could assert scholastic reasoning. But after all is said and done, the highest argument for believing God

37

preserved his word without error is the argument of faith.

"No, I cannot prove to you the King James Bible is the inerrant word of God. Neither can I prove to you Jesus saved my soul, and His Holy Spirit lives inside me. None of us can prove, to man's satisfaction, God's existence. Ultimately these truths are based on faith.

"Do you really believe the best God can do in preserving his words is to make them reliable or mostly true? Do you really believe God trusts his words to men, to human scholarship, without his omnipotent preservation?

Christians who believe mistakes exist in the bible: Are they more right with God than *Christians who believe the Bible is perfectly preserved?*

Psalms 12:6-7 King James Bible *The words of the LORD are pure words: as silver tried in a furnace of earth, purified seven times.* ***7*** *Thou shalt keep them, O LORD, thou shalt preserve them from this generation for ever.*

Readers are encouraged to compare Psalm 12:6-7 in other bible versions.

Suddenly there was a crack of lightning and the lights in the church went out.

"Please everyone, remain calm!" Burehc yelled compensating for the loss of the microphone. Immediately ushers opened the rear doors allowing

38

the waning evening's light to seep into the auditorium. "Due to the loss of power, we shall end this meeting. Our discussion continues next Saturday. I thank you all for coming and I look forward to seeing you again. Please exit the building slowly and cautiously."

Sunday morning Pastor Antipas did not attend his church. The associate pastor handled the sermon. After the service, he and a deacon drove to Pastor Antipas' house. By Monday, the heinous crime was covered in the local newspapers.

Margaret Thompson read the headlines in the bakery as she waited for Frank to wrap her coffee cake. "This is just the kind of thing Reverend Burehc talked about," she said.

"Sure is," said Frank shaking his head. "It's terrible, that's what it is. When something like this happens so close to home, it makes me feel sick right in my stomach. It's a good thing his wife was out of town."

"And to think it happened to a minister. What kind of a person would do such a thing?" said Margaret shuddering.

"The police think he startled a thief," said Frank, "But who knows? These days' people kill and destroy just for fun."

"I'll stop by the funeral home tomorrow and pay my respects," said Margaret.

"You won't see the body," said Frank. "With the decapitation and all, you know they'll keep the casket closed."

Revelation 2:28-29 *And I will give him the morning star.* *29* *He that hath an ear, let him hear what the Spirit saith unto the churches.*

End

Luciferian Society: Glossary

Story notes: Allegorical basis for characters: Subjective interpretation.

Alexander: "man defender"

Coppersmith (Professor): Apostle Paul's enemy. Enemy to God's words

2 Timothy 4:14-15 *Alexander the coppersmith did me much evil: the Lord reward him according to his works: 15 Of whom be thou ware also; for he hath greatly withstood our words.*

Antipas: 'against all' (who oppose God's preserved words)

Revelation 2:13 *I know thy works, and where thou dwellest, even where Satan's seat is: and thou holdest fast my name, and hast not denied my faith, even in those days wherein Antipas was my faithful martyr, who was slain among you, where Satan dwelleth.*

Revelation 20:4 *And I saw thrones, and they sat upon them, and judgment was given unto them: and I saw the souls of them that were beheaded for the witness of Jesus, and for the word of God, and which had not worshipped the beast, neither his image, neither had received his mark upon their foreheads, or in their hands; and they lived and reigned with Christ a thousand years.,....*

Babylon: literally means to confuse by mixing-consider hundreds of bible versions.

Burehc: is cherub spelled backward

Dan tribe in apostasy (Judges 18)

1 Kings 12:28-29 Whereupon the king took counsel, and made two calves of gold, and said unto them, It is too much for you to go up to Jerusalem: behold thy gods, O Israel, which brought thee up out of the land of Egypt. 29 And he set the one in Bethel, and the other put he in Dan.

Demetrius 'of Mother earth' Pastor of new age temple.

Acts 19:24 For a certain man named Demetrius, a silversmith, which made silver shrines for Diana, brought no small gain unto the craftsmen;

Dr.**Jehudi:**'he will be praised'

King Jehoiakim's servant and sycophant-delights in cutting out the words of God. His character seems most comfortable when higher authorities command the editing.

Jeremiah 36:21-24 So the king sent Jehudi to fetch the roll: and he took it out of Elishama the scribe's chamber. And Jehudi read it in the ears of the king, and in the ears of all the princes which stood beside the king. 22 Now the king sat in the winterhouse in the ninth month: and there was a fire on the hearth burning before him. 23 And it came to pass, that when Jehudi had read three or four leaves, *he cut it with the penknife, and cast it into the fire that was on the hearth, until all the roll was consumed in the fire that was on the hearth. **24** Yet they were not afraid, nor rent their garments, neither the king, nor any of his servants that heard all these words.*

Father **Micah:** 'who is like Jehovah?'

***Judges 17:5** And the man Micah had an house of gods, and made an ephod, and teraphim, and consecrated one of his sons, who became his priest.*

***Judges 17:10** And Micah said unto him, Dwell with me, and be unto me a father and a priest, and I will give thee ten shekels of silver by the year, and a suit of apparel, and thy victuals. So the Levite went in.*

Pastor **Leaven**: leaven 'typifies sin'

***1 Corinthians 5:7-8** Purge out therefore the old leaven, that ye may be a new lump, as ye are unleavened. For even Christ our passover is sacrificed for us: **8** Therefore let us keep the feast, not with old leaven, neither with the leaven of malice and wickedness; but with the unleavened bread of sincerity and truth.*

Malchus: 'kingly' a minister

***John 18:10** Then Simon Peter having a sword drew it, and smote the high priest's servant, and cut off his right ear. The servant's name was Malchus.*

Onyx: 'justifying or making equal' Master church road address

*Ezekiel 28:13-14 Thou hast been in Eden the garden of God; every precious stone was thy covering, the sardius, topaz, and the diamond, the beryl, **the onyx,** and the jasper, the sapphire, the emerald, and the carbuncle, and gold: the workmanship of thy tabrets and of thy pipes was prepared in thee in the day that thou wast created. **14** Thou art the anointed cherub that covereth; and I have set thee so: thou wast upon the holy mountain of God; thou hast walked up and down in the midst of the stones of fire.*

Books by Joseph Dulmage

Angels, Giants, and Things under the Earth
Approaching Adventure;
Distress of Souls
Divorce and Remarriage, For Christians
GAP
Kings Rule
Leviathan's Nightmare
Luciferian Society & The Wall
Serious and Unusual Christian Fiction
Tongues
What Might this Parable Be?

Made in the USA
Columbia, SC
13 June 2024

36546623R00026